The Ultimate Guide Volleyball For Beginners

Get Started Playing And Winning At Volleyball

DEDICATION

Contents

Introduction of Volleyball

Volleyball is a team sport in which two teams of six players are separated by a net. Each team tries to score points by grounding a ball on the other team's court under organized rules. It has been a part of the official program of the Summer Olympic Games since Tokyo 1964. Beach volleyball was introduced to the programme at the Atlanta 1996. The adapted version of volleyball at the Summer Paralympic Games is sitting volleyball.

The complete set of rules is extensive, but play essentially proceeds as follows: a player on one of the teams begins a 'rally' by serving the ball (tossing or releasing it and then hitting it with a hand or arm), from behind the back boundary line of the court, over the net, and into the receiving team's court. The receiving team must not let the ball be grounded within their court. The team may touch the ball up to three times to return the ball to the other side of the court, but individual players may not touch the ball twice consecutively. Typically, the first two touches are used to set up for an attack. An attack is an attempt to direct the ball back over the net in such a way that the team receiving the ball is unable to pass the ball and continue the rally, thus, losing the point. The team that wins the rally is awarded a point and serves the ball to start the next rally. A few of the most common faults include:

- Causing the ball to touch the ground or floor outside the opponents' court or without first passing over the net;
- Catching and throwing the ball;
- Double hit: two consecutive contacts with the ball made by the same player;

- Four consecutive contacts with the ball made by the same team;
- Net foul: touching the net during play;
- Foot fault: the foot crosses over the boundary line when serving.

The ball is usually played with the hands or arms, but players can legally strike or push (short contact) the ball with any part of the body.

A number of consistent techniques have evolved in volleyball, including spiking and blocking (because these plays are made above the top of the net, the vertical jump is an athletic skill emphasized in the sport) as well as passing, setting, and specialized player positions and offensive and defensive structures.

History of Volleyball

Origins

William G. Morgan, c. 1915

In the winter of 1895, in Holyoke, Massachusetts (United States),

William G. Morgan, a YMCA physical education director, created a new game called Mintonette, a name derived from the game of badminton, as a pastime to be played (preferably) indoors and by any number of players. The game took some of its characteristics from other sports such as baseball, tennis and handball. Another indoor sport, basketball, was catching on in the area, having been invented just ten miles (sixteen kilometres) away in the city of Springfield, Massachusetts, only four years before. Mintonette was designed to be an indoor sport, less rough than basketball, for older members of the YMCA, while still requiring a bit of athletic effort.

The first rules, written down by William G. Morgan, called for a net 6 ft 6 in (1.98 m) high, a 25 ft × 50 ft (7.6 m × 15.2 m) court, and any number of players. A match was composed of nine innings with three serves for each team in each inning, and no limit to the number of ball contacts for each team before sending the ball to the opponents' court. In case of a serving error, a second try was allowed. Hitting the ball into the net was considered a foul (with loss of the point or a side-out)——except in the case of the first-try serve.

After an observer, Alfred Halstead, noticed the volleying nature of the game at its first exhibition match in 1896, played at the International YMCA Training School (now called Springfield College), the game quickly became known as volleyball (it was originally spelled as two words: "volley ball"). Volleyball rules were slightly modified by the International YMCA Training School and the game spread around the country to various YMCAs.

In the early 1900s Spalding, through its publishing company American Sports Publishing Company, produced books with complete instruction and rules for the sport.

Refinements and later developments

Japanese American women playing volleyball, Manzanar internment camp, California, c. 1943

The first official ball used in volleyball is disputed; some sources say Spalding created the first official ball in 1896, while others claim it was created in 1900. The rules evolved over time: in 1916, in the Philippines, the skill and power of the set and spike had been introduced, and four years later a "three hits" rule and a rule against hitting from the back row were established. In 1917, the game was changed from requiring 21 points to win to a smaller 15 points to win. In 1919, about 16,000 volleyballs were distributed by the American Expeditionary Forces to their troops and allies, which sparked the growth of volleyball in new countries.

The first country outside the United States to adopt volleyball was Canada in 1900. An international federation, the Fédération Internationale de Volleyball (FIVB), was founded in 1947, and the first World Championships were held in 1949 for men and 1952 for women. The sport is now popular in Brazil, in Europe (where especially Italy, the Netherlands, and countries from Eastern Europe have been major forces since the late 1980s), in Russia, and in other countries including China and the rest of Asia, as well as in the United States.

Beach volleyball, a variation of the game played on sand and with only two players per team, became a FIVB-endorsed variation in

1987 and was added to the Olympic program at the 1996 Summer Olympics. Volleyball is also a sport at the Paralympics managed by the World Organization Volleyball for Disabled.

Nudists were early adopters of the game with regular organized play in clubs as early as the late 1920s. By the 1960s, a volleyball court had become standard in almost all nudist/naturist clubs.

Volleyball in the Olympics

Volleyball has been part of the Summer Olympics program for both men and women consistently since 1964.

Rules Of The Game

Volleyball court

The court dimensions

A volleyball court is 9 m × 18 m (29.5 ft × 59.1 ft), divided into equal square halves by a net with a width of one meter (39.4 in). The top of the net is 2.43 m (7 ft 11+11/16 in) above the center of the court for men's competition, and 2.24 m (7 ft 4+3/16 in) for women's competition, varied for veterans and junior competitions.

The minimum height clearance for indoor volleyball courts is 7 m (23.0 ft), although a clearance of 8 m (26.2 ft) is recommended.

A line 3 m (9.8 ft) from and parallel to the net is considered the "attack line". This "3 meter" (or "10-foot") line divides the court into "back row" and "front row" areas (also back court and front court). These are in turn divided into 3 areas each: these are numbered as follows, starting from area "1", which is the position of the serving player:

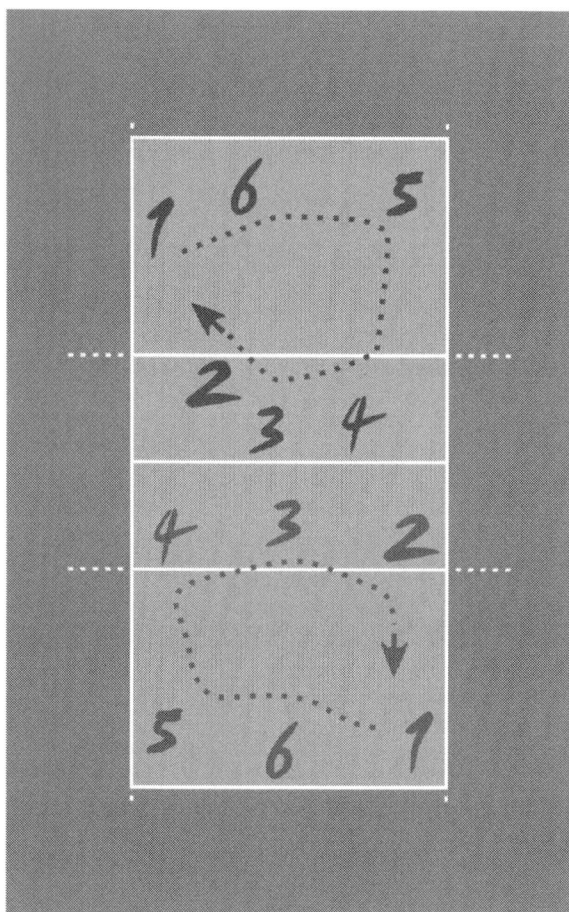

Rotation pattern

After a team gains the serve (also known as siding out), its members must rotate in a clockwise direction, with the player previously in area

"2" moving to area "1" and so on, with the player from area "1" moving to area "6". Each player rotates only one time after the team gains possession of the service; the next time each player rotates will be after the other team wins possession of the ball and loses the point.

The team courts are surrounded by an area called the free zone which is a minimum of 3 meters wide and which the players may enter and play within after the service of the ball. All lines denoting the boundaries of the team court and the attack zone are drawn or painted within the dimensions of the area and are therefore a part of the court or zone. If a ball comes in contact with the line, the ball is considered to be "in". An antenna is placed on each side of the net perpendicular to the sideline and is a vertical extension of the side boundary of the court. A ball passing over the net must pass completely between the antennae (or their theoretical extensions to the ceiling) without contacting them.

The ball

FIVB regulations state that the ball must be spherical, made of leather or synthetic leather, have a circumference of 65–67 cm (26–26 in), a weight of 260–280 g (9.2–9.9 oz) and an interior air pressure of 0.30–0.325 kg/cm2 0.30–0.325 kg/cm2 (4.27–4.62 psi). Other governing bodies have similar regulations.

Gameplay

White is on the attack while red attempts to block.

Each team consists of six players. To get play started, a team is chosen to serve by coin toss. A player from the serving team throws the ball into the air and attempts to hit the ball so it passes over the net on a course such that it will land in the opposing team's court (the serve). The opposing team must use a combination of no more than three contacts with the volleyball to return the ball to the opponent's side of the net. These contacts usually consist first of the bump or pass so that the ball's trajectory is aimed towards the player designated as the setter; second of the set (usually an over-hand pass using wrists to push finger-tips at the ball) by the setter so that the ball's trajectory is aimed towards a spot where one of the players designated as an attacker can hit it, and third by the attacker who spikes (jumping, raising one arm above the head and hitting the ball so it will move quickly down to the ground on the opponent's court) to return the ball over the net. The team with possession of the ball that is trying to attack the ball as described is said to be on offence.

The team on defence attempts to prevent the attacker from directing the ball into their court: players at the net jump and reach above the top (and if possible, across the plane) of the net to block the attacked ball. If the ball is hit around, above, or through the block, the defensive players arranged in the rest of the court attempt to control the ball with a dig (usually a fore-arm pass of a hard-driven ball). After a successful dig, the team transitions to offence.

Buddhist monks play volleyball in the Himalayan state of Sikkim, India.

The game continues in this manner, rallying back and forth until the ball touches the court within the boundaries or until an error is made. The most frequent errors that are made are either to fail to return the ball over the net within the allowed three touches, or to cause the ball to land outside the court. A ball is "in" if any part of it touches the inside of a team's court or a sideline or end-line, and a strong spike may compress the ball enough when it lands that a ball which at first appears to be going out may actually be in. Players may travel well outside the court to play a ball that has gone over a sideline or end-line in the air.

Other common errors include a player touching the ball twice in succession, a player "catching" the ball, a player touching the net while attempting to play the ball, or a player penetrating under the net into the opponent's court. There are a large number of other errors specified in the rules, although most of them are infrequent occurrences. These errors include back-row or libero players spiking the ball or blocking (back-row players may spike the ball if they jump from behind the attack line), players not being in the correct position when the ball is served, attacking the serve in the frontcourt and above the height of the net, using another player as a source of support to reach the ball, stepping over the back boundary line when serving, taking more than 8 seconds to serve, or playing the ball when it is above the opponent's court.

Scoring

Scorer's table just before a game

A point is scored when the ball contacts the floor within the court boundaries or when an error is made: when the ball strikes one team's side of the court, the other team gains a point; and when an error is made, the team that did not make the error is awarded a point, in either case paying no regard to whether they served the ball or not. If any part of the ball hits the line, the ball is counted as in the court.

The team that won the point serves for the next point. If the team that won the point served in the previous point, the same player serves again. If the team that won the point did not serve the previous point, the players of the team acquiring the serve rotate their position on the court in a clockwise manner. The game continues, with the first team to score 25 points by a two-point margin awarded the set. Matches are best-of-five sets and the fifth set, if necessary, is usually played to 15 points. (Scoring differs between leagues, tournaments, and levels; high schools sometimes play best-of-three to 25; in the NCAA matches are played best-of-five to 25 as of the 2008 season.)

Before 1999, points could be scored only when a team had the serve (side-out scoring) and all sets went up to only 15 points. The FIVB changed the rules in 1999 (with the changes being compulsory in 2000) to use the current scoring system (formerly known as rally point system), primarily to make the length of the match more predictable and to make the game more spectator- and television-friendly.

The final year of side-out scoring at the NCAA Division I Women's Volleyball Championship was 2000. Rally point scoring debuted in 2001, and games were played to 30 points through 2007. For the 2008 season, games were renamed "sets" and reduced to 25 points to win. Most high schools in the U.S. changed to rally scoring in 2003, and several states implemented it the previous year on an experimental basis.

Libero

The libero player was introduced internationally in 1998, and made its debut for NCAA competition in 2002. The libero is a player specialized in defensive skills: the libero must wear a contrasting jersey color from their teammates and cannot block or attack the ball when it is entirely above net height. When the ball is not in play, the libero can replace any back-row player, without prior notice to the officials. This replacement does not count against the substitution limit each team is allowed per set, although the libero may be replaced only by the player whom he or she replaced. Most U.S. high schools added the libero position from 2003 to 2005.

The modern-day libero often takes on the role of a second setter. When the setter digs the ball, the libero is typically responsible for the second ball and sets to the front row attacker. The libero may function as a setter only under certain restrictions. To make an overhand set, the libero must be standing behind (and not stepping on) the 3-meter line; otherwise, the ball cannot be attacked above the net in front of the 3-meter line. An underhand pass is allowed from any part of the court.

The libero is, generally, the most skilled defensive player on the team. There is also a libero tracking sheet, where the referees or officiating team must keep track of whom the libero subs in and out for. Under FIVB (Federation Internationale de Volleyball) rules, two liberos are designated at the beginning of the play, only one of whom can be on the court at any time.

Furthermore, a libero is not allowed to serve, according to international rules. NCAA rules for both men and women differ on this point; a 2004 rule change allows the libero to serve, but only in a specific rotation. That is, the libero can only serve for one person, not for all of the people for whom he or she goes in. That rule change was also applied to high school and junior high play soon after.

Recent rule changes

Other rule changes enacted in 2000 include allowing serves in which the ball touches the net, as long as it goes over the net into the opponents' court. Also, the service area was expanded to allow players to serve from anywhere behind the end line but still within the theoretical extension of the sidelines. Other changes were made to lighten up calls on faults for carries and double-touches, such as allowing multiple contacts by a single player ("double-hits") on a team's first contact provided that they are a part of a single play on the ball.

In 2008, the NCAA changed the minimum number of points needed to win any of the first four sets from 30 to 25 for women's volleyball (men's volleyball remained at 30 for another three years, switching to 25 in 2011). If a fifth (deciding) set is reached, the minimum required score remains at 15. In addition, the word "game" is now referred to as "set".

The Official Volleyball Rules are prepared and updated every few years by the FIVB's Rules of the Game and Refereeing Commission. The latest edition is usually available on the FIVB's website.

Skills

Competitive teams master six basic skills: serve, pass, set, attack, block and dig. Each of these skills comprises a number of specific techniques that have been introduced over the years and are now considered standard practice in high-level volleyball.

Serve

A player making a jump serve

A player stands behind the inline and serves the ball, in an attempt to drive it into the opponent's court. The main objective is to make it land inside the court; it is also desirable to set the ball's direction, speed and acceleration so that it becomes difficult for the receiver to handle it properly. A serve is called an "ace" when the ball lands directly onto the court or travels outside the court after being touched by an opponent; when the only player on the server's team to touch the ball is the server.

In contemporary volleyball, many types of serves are employed:

- Underhand: a serve in which the player strikes the ball below the waist instead of tossing it up and striking it with an overhand throwing motion. Underhand serves are considered very easy to receive and are rarely employed in high-level competitions.

- Sky ball serve: a specific type of underhand serve occasionally used in beach volleyball, where the ball is hit so high it comes down almost in a straight line. This serve was invented and employed almost exclusively by the Brazilian team in the early 1980s and is now considered outdated. During the 2016 Olympic Games in Rio de Janeiro, however, the sky ball serve was extensively played by Italian beach volleyball player Adrian Carambula. In Brazil, this serve is called Jornada nas Estrelas (Star Trek)

- Topspin: an overhand serve where the player tosses the ball high and hits it with a wrist snap, giving it topspin which causes it to drop faster than it would otherwise and helps maintain a straight flight path. Topspin serves are generally hit hard and aimed at a specific returner or part of the court. Standing topspin serves are rarely used above the high school level of play.

- Float: an overhand serve where the ball is hit with no spin so that its path becomes unpredictable, akin to a knuckleball in baseball.

- Jump serve: an overhand serve where the ball is first tossed high in the air, then the player makes a timed approach and jumps to make contact with the ball, hitting it with much pace and topspin. This is the most popular serve among college and professional teams.

- Jump float: an overhand serve where the ball is tossed high enough that the player may jump before hitting it similarly to a standing float serve. The ball is tossed lower than a topspin jump serve, but contact is still made while in the air. This serve is becoming more popular among college and professional players because it has a certain unpredictability in its flight pattern.

Pass

Also called reception, the pass is the attempt by a team to properly handle the opponent's serve or any form of attack. Proper handling includes not only preventing the ball from touching the court but also making it reach the position where the setter is standing quickly and precisely.

The skill of passing involves fundamentally two specific techniques: underarm pass, or bump, where the ball touches the inside part of the joined forearms or platform, at waistline; and overhand pass, where it is handled with the fingertips, like a set, above the head. Either are acceptable in professional and beach volleyball; however, there are much tighter regulations on the overhand pass in beach volleyball. When a player passes a ball to their setter, it's ideal that the ball does not have a lot of spin to make it easier for the setter.

Set

Jump set

The set is usually the second contact that a team makes with the ball. The main goal of setting is to put the ball in the air in such a way that it can be driven by an attack into the opponent's court. The setter coordinates the offensive movements of a team, and is the player who ultimately decides which player will actually attack the ball.

As with passing, one may distinguish between an overhand and a bump set. Since the former allows for more control over the speed and direction of the ball, the bump is used only when the ball is so low it cannot be properly handled with fingertips, or in beach volleyball where rules regulating overhand setting are more stringent. In the case of a set, one also speaks of a front or back set, meaning whether the ball is passed in the direction the setter is facing or behind the setter. There is also a jump set that is used when the ball is too close to the net. In this case, the setter usually jumps off their right foot straight up to avoid going into the net. The setter usually stands about ⅔ of the way from the left to the right of the net and faces the left (the larger portion of net that he or she can see).

Sometimes a setter refrains from raising the ball for a teammate to perform an attack and tries to play it directly onto the opponent's court. This movement is called a "dump". This can only be performed when the setter is in the front row, otherwise it constitutes an illegal back court attack. The most common dumps are to 'throw' the ball behind the setter or in front of the setter to zones 2 and 4. More experienced setters toss the ball into the deep corners or spike the ball on the second hit.

As with a set or an overhand pass, the setter/passer must be careful to touch the ball with both hands at the same time. If one hand is noticeably late to touch the ball this could result in a less effective set, as well as the referee calling a 'double hit' and giving the point to the opposing team.

Attack

A Spanish player, #18 in red outfit, about to spike towards the Portuguese field, whose players try to block the way

The attack, also known as the spike, is usually the third contact a team makes with the ball. The object of attacking is to handle the ball so that it lands on the opponent's court and cannot be defended. A player makes a series of steps (the "approach"), jumps, and swings at

31

the ball.

Ideally, the contact with the ball is made at the apex of the hitter's jump. At the moment of contact, the hitter's arm is fully extended above their head and slightly forward, making the highest possible contact while maintaining the ability to deliver a powerful hit. The hitter uses arm swing, wrist snap, and a rapid forward contraction of the entire body to drive the ball. A 'bounce' is a slang term for a very hard/loud spike that follows an almost straight trajectory steeply downward into the opponent's court and bounces very high into the air. A "kill" is the slang term for an attack that is not returned by the other team thus resulting in a point.

Contemporary volleyball comprises a number of attacking techniques:

- Backcourt (or back row): an attack performed by a back-row player. The player must jump from behind the 3-meter line before making contact with the ball, but may land in front of the 3-meter line. A Pipe Attack is when the center player in the back row attacks the ball.

- Line and Cross-court Shot: refers to whether the ball flies in a straight trajectory parallel to the sidelines, or crosses through the court in an angle. A cross-court shot with a very pronounced angle, resulting in the ball landing near the 3-meter line, is called a cut shot.

- Dip/Dink/Tip/Cheat/Dump: the player does not try to make a hit, but touches the ball lightly, so that it lands on an area of the opponent's court that is not being covered by the defence.

- Tool/Wipe/Block-abuse: the player does not try to make a hard spike, but hits the ball so that it touches the opponent's block and then bounces off-court.

- Off-speed hit: the player does not hit the ball hard, reducing its speed and thus confusing the opponent's defence.

- Quick hit/"One": an attack (usually by the middle blocker) where the approach and jump begin before the setter contacts the ball. The set (called a "quick set") is placed only slightly above the net and the ball is struck by the hitter almost immediately after leaving the setter's hands. Quick attacks are often effective because they isolate the middle blocker to be the only blocker on the hit.

- Slide: a variation of the quick hit that uses a low backset. The middle hitter steps around the setter and hits from behind him or her.

- Double quick hit/"Stack"/"Tandem": a variation of quick hit where two hitters, one in front and one behind the setter or both in front of the setter, jump to perform a quick hit at the same time. It can be used to deceive opposite blockers and free a fourth hitter attacking from back-court, maybe without block at all.

Block

Three players performing a block (a.k.a. triple block)

Blocking refers to the actions taken by players standing at the net to stop or alter an opponent's attack.

A block that is aimed at completely stopping an attack, thus making the ball remain in the opponent's court, is called offensive. A well-executed offensive block is performed by jumping and reaching to penetrate with one's arms and hands over the net and into the opponent's area. It requires anticipating the direction the ball will go once the attack takes place. It may also require calculating the best footwork to executing the "perfect" block.

The jump should be timed so as to intercept the ball's trajectory prior to it crossing over the plane of the net. Palms are held deflected downward roughly 45–60 degrees toward the interior of the opponents' court. A "roof" is a spectacular offensive block that redirects the power and speed of the attack straight down to the attacker's floor as if the attacker hit the ball into the underside of a peaked house roof.

By contrast, it is called a defensive, or "soft" block if the goal is to control and deflect the hard-driven ball up so that it slows down and becomes easier to defend. A well-executed soft-block is performed by jumping and placing one's hands above the net with no penetration into the opponent's court and with the palms up and fingers pointing backwards.

Blocking is also classified according to the number of players involved. Thus, one may speak of single (or solo), double, or triple block.

Successful blocking does not always result in a "roof" and many times does not even touch the ball. While it is obvious that a block was a success when the attacker is roofed, a block that consistently forces the attacker away from their 'power' or preferred attack into a more easily controlled shot by the defence is also a highly successful block.

At the same time, the block position influences the positions where other defenders place themselves while opponent hitters are spiking.

Dig

Digging is the ability to prevent the ball from touching one's court after a spike or attack, particularly a ball that is nearly touching the ground. In many aspects, this skill is similar to passing, or bumping: overhand dig and bump are also used to distinguish between defensive actions taken with fingertips or with joined arms. It varies from passing however in that is it a much more reflex based skill, especially at the higher levels. It is especially important while digging for players to stay on their toes; several players choose to employ a split step to make sure they're ready to move in any direction.

Some specific techniques are more common in digging than in passing. A player may sometimes perform a "dive", i.e., throw their body in the air with a forward movement in an attempt to save the ball, and land on their chest. When the player also slides their hand under a ball that is almost touching the court, this is called a "pancake". The pancake is frequently used in indoor volleyball, but rarely if ever in beach volleyball because the uneven and yielding nature of the sand court limits the chances that the ball will make good, clean contact with the hand. When used correctly, it is one of the more spectacular defensive volleyball plays.

Sometimes a player may also be forced to drop their body quickly to the floor to save the ball. In this situation, the player makes use of a specific rolling technique to minimize the chances of injuries.

Team play

U.S. women's team doing team planning

Volleyball is essentially a game of transition from one of the above skills to the next, with choreographed team movement between plays on the ball. These team movements are determined by the teams chosen serve receive system, offensive system, coverage system, and defensive system.

The serve-receive system is the formation used by the receiving team to attempt to pass the ball to the designated setter. Systems can consist of 5 receivers, 4 receivers, 3 receivers, and in some cases 2 receivers. The most popular formation at higher levels is a 3 receiver formation consisting of two left sides and a libero receiving every rotation. This allows middles and right sides to become more specialized at hitting and blocking.

Offensive systems are the formations used by the offence to attempt to ground the ball into the opposing court (or otherwise score points). Formations often include designated player positions with skill specialization. Popular formations include the 4–2, 6–2, and 5-1 systems. There are also several different attacking schemes teams can use to keep the opposing defence off balance.

Coverage systems are the formations used by the offence to protect their court in the case of a blocked attack. Executed by the 5 offensive players not directly attacking the ball, players move to assigned positions around the attacker to dig up any ball that deflects off the block back into their own court. Popular formations include the 2-3 system and the 1-2-2 system. In lieu of a system, some teams just use a random coverage with the players nearest the hitter.

Defensive systems are the formations used by the defence to protect against the ball being grounded into their court by the opposing team. The system will outline which players are responsible for which areas of the court depending on where the opposing team is attacking from. Popular systems include the 6-Up, 6-Back-Deep, and 6-Back-Slide defence. There are also several different blocking schemes teams can employ to disrupt the opposing teams' offence.

When one player is ready to serve, some teams will line up their other five players in a screen to obscure the view of the receiving team. This action is only illegal if the server makes use of the screen, so the call is made at the referee's discretion as to the impact the screen made on the receiving team's ability to pass the ball. The most common style of screening involves a W formation designed to take up as much horizontal space as possible.

Strategy

Player specialization

There are five positions filled on every volleyball team at the elite level. Setter, Outside Hitter/Left Side Hitter, Middle Hitter, Opposite Hitter/Right Side Hitter and Libero/Defensive Specialist. Each of these positions plays a specific, key role in winning a volleyball match.

- Setters have the task for orchestrating the offence of the team. They aim for the second touch and their main responsibility is to place the ball in the air where the attackers can place the ball into the opponents' court for a point. They have to be able to operate with the hitters, manage the tempo of their side of the court and choose the right attackers to set. Setters need to have a swift and skilful appraisal and tactical accuracy and must be quick at moving around the court. At elite level, setters used to usually be the shortest players of a team (before liberos were introduced), not being typically required to perform jump hits, but that would imply need for short-term replacemente by taller bench players when critical points required more effective blocks; in the 1990s taller setters (e.g. Fabio Vullo, Peter Blangé) became being deployed, in order to improve blocks.

- Liberos are defensive players who are responsible for receiving the attack or serve. They are usually the players on the court with the quickest reaction time and best passing skills. Libero means 'free' in Italian—they receive this name as they have the ability to substitute for any other player on the court during each play. They do not necessarily need to be tall, as they never play at the net, which allows shorter players with strong passing and defensive skills to excel in the position and play an important role in the team's success. A player designated as a libero for a match may not play other roles during that match. Liberos wear a different colour jersey than their teammates.

- Middle blockers or Middle hitters are players that can perform very fast attacks that usually take place near the setter. They are specialized in blocking since they must attempt to stop equally fast plays from their opponents and then quickly set up a double block at the sides of the court. In non-beginners play, every team will have two middle hitters. At elite levels, middle hitters are usually the tallest players, whose limited agility is countered by their height enabling more effective blocks.

- Outside hitters or Left side hitters attack from near the left antenna. The outside hitter is usually the most consistent hitter on the team and gets the most sets. Inaccurate first passes usually result in a set to the outside hitter rather than middle or opposite. Since most sets to the outside are high, the outside hitter may take a longer approach, always starting from outside the court sideline. In non-beginners play, there are again two outside hitters on every team in every match. At elite level, outside hitters are slightly shorter than middle hitters and outside hitters, but have the best defensive skills, therefore always re-placing to the middle while in the back row.

- Opposite hitters or Right-side hitters carry the defensive workload for a volleyball team in the front row. Their primary responsibilities are to put up a well-formed block against the opponents' Outside Hitters and serve as a backup setter. Sets to the opposite usually go to the right side of the antennae. Therefore, they are usually the most technical hitters since balls lifted to the right side are quicker and more difficult to handle (the setters having to place the ball while slightly off-set to the right, and with their back to the attacker), and also having to jump from the back row when the setter is on the front row. At elite level, until the 1990s several opposite hitters used to be able to also play as middle hitters (e.g. Andrea Zorzi, Andrea Giani), before high specialization curtained this flexibility in the role.

At some levels where substitutions are unlimited, teams will make use of a Defensive Specialist in place of or in addition to a Libero. This position does not have unique rules like the libero position, instead, these players are used to substitute out a poor back row defender using regular substitution rules. A defensive specialist is often used if you have a particularly poor back court defender in right side or left side, but your team is already using a libero to take out your middles. Most often, the situation involves a team using a right side player with a big block who must be subbed out in the back row because they aren't able to effectively play backcourt defence. Similarly, teams might use a Serving Specialist to sub out a poor server.

Formations

The three standard volleyball formations are known as "4–2", "6–2" and "5–1", which refers to the number of hitters and setters respectively. 4–2 is a basic formation used only in beginners' play, while 5–1 is by far the most common formation in high-level play.

4–2

The 4–2 formation has four hitters and two setters. The setters usually set from the middle front or right front position. The team will, therefore, have two front-row attackers at all times. In the international 4–2, the setters set from the right front position. The international 4–2 translates more easily into other forms of offence.

The setters line up opposite each other in the rotation. The typical lineup has two outside hitters. By aligning like positions opposite themselves in the rotation, there will always be one of each position in the front and back rows. After service, the players in the front row move into their assigned positions, so that the setter is always in the middle front. Alternatively, the setter moves into the right front and has both a middle and an outside attacker; the disadvantage here lies in the lack of an offside hitter, allowing one of the other team's blockers to "cheat in" on a middle block.

The clear disadvantage to this offensive formation is that there are only two attackers, leaving a team with fewer offensive weapons.

Another aspect is to see the setter as an attacking force, albeit a weakened force, because when the setter is in the frontcourt they are able to 'tip' or 'dump', so when the ball is close to the net on the second touch, the setter may opt to hit the ball over with one hand. This means that the blocker who would otherwise not have to block the setter is engaged and may allow one of the hitters to have an easier attack.

6–2

In the 6–2 formation, a player always comes forward from the back row to set. The three front row players are all in attacking positions. Thus, all six players act as hitters at one time or another, while two can act as setters. So the 6–2 formation is actually a 4–2 system, but the back-row setter penetrates to set.

The 6–2 lineup thus requires two setters, who line up opposite to each other in the rotation. In addition to the setters, a typical lineup will have two middle hitters and two outside hitters. By aligning like positions opposite themselves in the rotation, there will always be one of each position in the front and back rows. After service, the players in the front row move into their assigned positions.

The advantage of the 6–2 is that there are always three front-row hitters available, maximizing the offensive possibilities. However, not only does the 6–2 require a team to possess two people capable of performing the highly specialized role of setter, it also requires both of those players to be effective offensive hitters when not in the setter position. At the international level, only the Cuban National Women's Team employs this kind of formation. It is also used by NCAA teams in Division III men's play and women's play in all divisions, partially due to the variant rules used which allow more substitutions per set than the 6 allowed in the standard rules—12 in matches involving two Division III men's teams and 15 for all women's play.

5–1

The 5–1 formation has only one player who assumes setting responsibilities regardless of their position in the rotation. The team will, therefore, have three front-row attackers when the setter is in the back row and only two when the setter is in the front row, for a total of five possible attackers.

The player opposite the setter in a 5–1 rotation is called the opposite hitter. In general, opposite hitters do not pass; they stand behind their teammates when the opponent is serving. The opposite hitter may be used as a third attack option (back-row attack) when the setter is in the front row: this is the normal option used to increase the attack capabilities of modern volleyball teams. Normally the opposite hitter is the most technically skilled hitter of the team. Back-row attacks generally come from the back-right position, known as zone 1, but are increasingly performed from back-centre in high-level play.

The big advantage of this system is that the setter always has 3 hitters to vary sets with. If the setter does this well, the opponent's middle blocker may not have enough time to block with the outside blocker, increasing the chance for the attacking team to make a point.

There is another advantage, the same as that of a 4–2 formation: when the setter is a front-row player, he or she is allowed to jump and "dump" the ball onto the opponent's side. This too can confuse the opponent's blocking players: the setter can jump and dump or can set to one of the hitters. A good setter knows this and thus won't only jump to dump or to set for a quick hit, but when setting outside as well to confuse the opponent.

The 5–1 offence is actually a mix of 6–2 and 4–2: when the setter is in the front row, the offense looks like a 4–2; when the setter is in the back row, the offense looks like a 6–2.

Controversies

In 2017, a new volleyball players' union was formed in response to dissatisfaction with the organization and structure of professional beach volleyball tournaments. The union is named the International Beach Volleyball Players Association, and it consists of almost 100 professional players. The IBVPA claims its goal is to help athletes and provide them with the means to enjoy playing volleyball by improving the way the sport is run.

Another controversy within the sport is the issue of the inclusion of transgender players. With transgender athletes such as Tiffany Abreu joining professional volleyball teams alongside other non-transgender teammates, many professionals, sports analysts, and fans of volleyball are either expressing concerns about the legitimacy and fairness of having transgender players on a team or expressing support for the transgender people's efforts.

Basic Volleyball Terminology

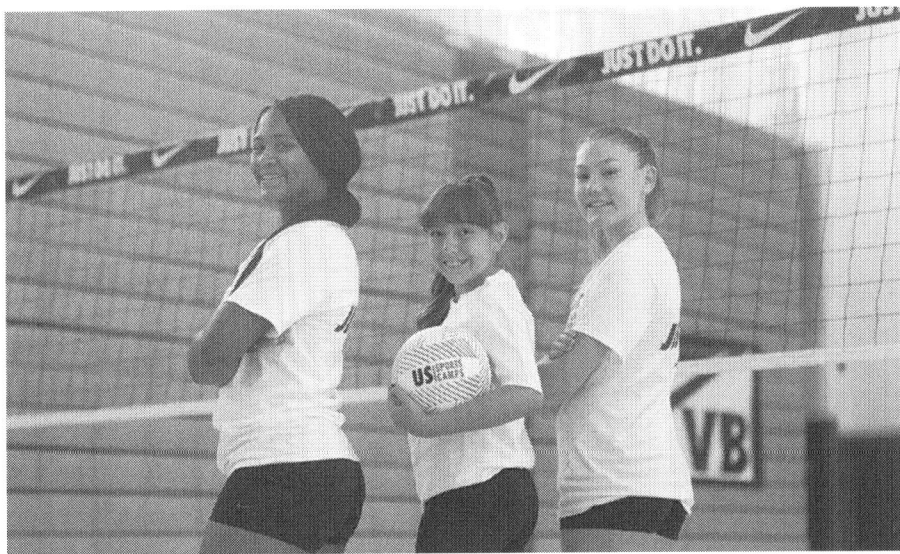

Like all sports, volleyball has some unique terminology that only people in the sport would understand, and as a first-year parent it can be a little intimidating at times. Understanding simple sayings and game terms is a great way to familiarize yourself with the world of volleyball. Here is a quick guide to some of the common words used in volleyball games and practices.

Ace: A serve that is not returned and results in a point.

Assist: Passing or setting the ball to a player who attacks the ball for a point.

Block: A defensive play, where a player deflects a spiked ball back into the opponent's court by jumping in front of the ball with their hands above the net.

Campfire: A ball that falls on the floor and is surrounded by two or more players. The moment it hits the floor it looks like the players are encircling the ball and starting a campfire.

Cut Shot: An attack with angle, almost parallel to the net.

Dig: Passing a spiked or rapidly hit ball.

Dink: A legal pushing of the ball over the blockers.

Double Hit: When a player makes contact with the ball twice in a row. This is considered an illegal hit.

Floater: A non-spinning serve, it can sometimes have erratic movement during flight.

Footfault: When a player steps over the line while serving, which results in a point for the opposing team.

Jump Serve: A type of serve that is done by tossing the ball into the air, jumping, and hitting the ball when it is in its downward motion.

Joust: When the ball is falling directly on top of the net, two opposing players will jump and attempt to push the ball to the other side.

Kill: A successful hit that results in an immediate point.

Let: When a serve hits the top of the net and rolls onto the other side, resulting in a point.

Line shot: A ball that is spiked right down the opposing sideline

Off-speed hit: A ball that is spiked with less force and has spin.

Power alley: A cross court spike that reaches the furthest end of the court.

Reception error: When a player is unable to return a serve that should have been returned, and it results in an ace.

Roll shot: An offensive play similar to a spike, but a hitter will make contact underneath the ball and move their arm upwards instead of swinging down. This type of shot is meant to go high enough to avoid a block and is typically aimed around 10 feet away from the net.

Pancake: A type of dig that occurs when a player extends his or her hand flat on the floor, and lets the ball bounce off the back of his or her hand.

Service error: An unsuccessful serve that occurs by the ball landing out of bounds, failing to clear the net, or a foot fault from the server.

Shank: A wild and unplayable pass.

Shot: An offensive play in which a ball is set and directed into an open area on the court.

Side out: When the serving team loses the rally causing the other team to serve for the next point.

Spike: When the hitter attacks the ball with a swinging motion. This is in an attempt to get a kill.

Strong side: Left side of the court for right handed hitters.

Tip: A soft and off-speed attack done with the fingertips.

Weak side: Right side of the court.

How To Play Volleyball

Packed with thrills, bumps, sets and spikes, volleyball is a brilliant spectator sport – but it's even better when you get stuck in yourself. This high-speed game requires athleticism, endurance and power.

If you're a beginner, there are plenty of ways to build up your skills and learn how to play volleyball – both indoor and beach. Say goodbye to the sidelines and hello to the adrenaline-packed court with this handy guide. We'll take you through the basics, cover the key moves to learn and give you top tips on how to develop your prowess on the court.

What are the basics of volleyball?

If you're thinking about taking up this exhilarating sport or just want to learn more, read through our basic rules on how to play volleyball. From team formations to how to score a point, we'll help you pick up the essential rules before you get started.

An indoor volleyball match is the best of five games. The team who takes the majority (three games) is the overall winner of the match. For beach volleyball, it's best of three.

To win a game, a team must score 25 points with a two-point difference. If they're too closely matched, the game can continue over the 25-point maximum. On the final deciding game of the match it's only played until 15 points, but the two-point difference still applies. In beach volleyball, a game is played to 21 points, with the same final round and tiebreak rule. You can find out more in our video guide to beach volleyball.

Each indoor volleyball team consists of six players, whereas beach volleyball is played in teams of two. For indoor volleyball, there are a number of positions. Usually, there are three players at the front near the net and another three towards the back of the court.

For the first game, the **teams will play a short volley to decide who will serve**. Then the loser of the previous game will serve for the duration of that game.

A rally begins with a serve. The server must take their shot from behind the end line and choose between an underhand or overhand shot. It's fine for the ball to graze the net, as long as the ball falls into the other side of the court.

A point is scored when a team wins a rally. Every rally begins with a serve and ends when a team wins a point. They do this in one of two ways. If your team sends the ball over the net and the defending team fail to return the ball, you score a point. You can also win a point if the other team hit the ball out of the designated court boundary. If a player on the other team makes a fault, it's also possible for your team to win a point.

Every time a team wins a point, they will rotate their position in a clockwise direction around the court.

A team can hit the ball to each other a maximum of three times before returning it to the other side of the court.

What are the positions in volleyball?

For beach volleyball, there are only two players per team. However, indoor volleyball is a little bit more complicated. Each team has six players, with three at the front in the attack zone and three in the back in the defence zone. Here's some information on who does what when playing volleyball:

Outside hitter: As you face the net, this player stands at the front-left of the court in the attack zone. Sometimes called the wing spiker, they often attack the ball a setter has prepared for them. While the ball is in play they can often work across the front and back row.

Right side hitter: This player has similar responsibilities to the outside hitter, but they focus on the right-hand side of the court.

Opposite hitter: This is the player who scores the most points in the game. Their position is usually in the back left corner of the court. Not only do they need to score points, but, because they play against the other team's opposite hitter, they need defensive skills too.

Setter: Often called the playmaker, this player is like the quarterback of the team. They run the offensive strategies and set the ball up for the attackers to score. They're often in the right-back of the court and can work both rows.

Middle blocker: Sitting in the middle, right in front of the net, this player's main responsibility is to block attacks from the other team. They're also a key passer who helps get the ball to the setter.

Libero: This is a back row player, who can only work at the rear of the court. They usually wear a different colour top to the rest of the team and can enter and exit the game without substitution. They also can replace any other player and often swaps places with the middle blocker.

What are the rules of indoor and beach volleyball?

Here are a few things you need to know to ensure you don't violate any rules or give the other team a point. You must not:

- Step on or over the end line when taking a serve

- Hit or serve the ball into the net

- Touch the net while the ball is in play

- Reach over the net to get the ball. You may reach over to execute a follow-through or block a returning ball

- Reach under the net

How to play volleyball: what are the moves?

There are a few ways you can play the ball in volleyball. Here are the main moves you can play to help you get started and understand what you can do to develop your game.

Beginners: When you first start off, it's a good idea to begin by catching and tossing the ball so to get a feel for the rules while keeping the ball in play for longer. Once you've mastered the rules and the flow, it's time to start bringing hits into the game. For an expert opinion, see what three-time gold medallist Karch Kiraly thinks are the qualities needed for volleyball success.

Passing: This is where a player receives the ball from the server and passes it to the playmaker. This is usually done with an underhand bump in a short, controlled manner, with minimal arm swing. It's quite literally a bump, rather than a hit.

Setting: The setter is the playmaker in volleyball. They prepare the ball so it's well-placed for an attacker to shoot and score a point for their team. Overhead setting is when a player places both their hands above their forehead, creating a triangle shape with their thumbs and index fingers. They push the ball up with their fingers, with the attacker ready to take their shot.

Spiking: This is one of the most impressive-looking moves in the game. A spike is generally when a player runs, jumps and hits the ball over the net with a powerful swing. Usually this is a move for an attacker or shooter, as these big hits usually win points. If you're a beginner, try to avoid spiking until you can maintain a long rally.

Blocking: A block is a defensive move used at the net. When an attacker moves to shoot, a maximum of three players on the other team come close to the net and jump just after the attacker with their arms up. When the ball comes over the net, it'll be blocked by the players and either move into their side or back towards the opposing team.

Digging: When the ball is heading towards the floor after an attack, a defender from the back row can run or dive forward to bump the ball back up and pass it to another team member.

16 Volleyball Tips For Beginners

1. Call mine, even when it seems obvious

One of the first things you learn in grade school volleyball is to call mine when you're in position to take the volleyball. As you play in higher levels of volleyball, this becomes engrained, and you automatically call mine, even when it seems pretty obvious.

For newer players, this instinct isn't as natural. If the ball is coming to you, of course you're going to get it! However, for some players, if they don't hear someone calling "mine", they may assume that the ball is still up for grabs – and someone needs to get it!

Calling "mine" might seem silly, but after you've played in a few games, you'll realize how common it actually is. So don't be afraid to speak up and call for that ball!

2. Try to use all three hits

In volleyball, each team gets to touch the ball three times before they have to send it back over the net. (Well, technically, they get 4 hits, if one of those touches was a block.) Regardless, sometimes more inexperienced players might get nervous or intimidated by the ball and send the ball over the net before their team has maximized their 3 hits.

Strategically, this could result in a missed scoring opportunity. The classic bump-set-spike play needs all three hits to be executed. So if a player is bumping the ball over the net with unused hits, they may be missing out on a scoring opportunity.

Having said that, sometimes hitting the ball on the second hit can be its own strategy and could result in a point. However, what I'm getting at here is that players should think about when to send the ball over the net to maximize the scoring opportunity for their team, and that's often using all three hits.

3. Don't touch the second ball – unless the setter has called for help

While we're on the topic of three touches, it's a good time to remind players to let the setter take that second ball. The setter is a specialized position that takes the second ball and sets up the hitters.

Sometimes that first bump can be off-target from where it's supposed to go, and the setter has to run it down. And sometimes, that ball might be headed right towards one of the other players. While it might be tempting to just set the ball, the setter is the specialized player whose role it is to setup the hitters.

And the thing with setters, is that they are usually FAST! They will very likely get to that second ball – after all, it's what they've been trained to do! Even when they're running to the ball, they will very likely be able to get a good set to one of the hitters.

However, they've also been trained to know when it makes more sense to let a teammate take that second ball, and that's when they'll call out, "help", signalling one of their teammates to step in and set instead. So, if the ball seems like it's heading right towards you, just keep an ear open for the setter's call of help, then step in and help out your teammate!

4. Don't set the ball too close to the net

If the setter calls help and a non-setter player ends up having to set the ball, one of the most common errors they make is to set the ball too close to the net. This means that the hitter doesn't get to use their full hitting approach, and their hitting options are more limited.

In addition to being tricky to hit, a set that is too close to the net can also be somewhat unsafe, especially for less experienced hitters or blockers. If a hitter isn't used to adjusting to a tight set, they may land in or under the net, potentially landing on the feet of the blockers. This is one of the most common ways of becoming injured in volleyball, often resulting in ankle or knee injuries.

Instead of aiming right for the net, aim for about a foot away from the net. Even if it's off target a little bit, this gives some buffer room. The hitter shouldn't be expecting a perfect set from a non-setter player anyway, so they should be ready to adjust.

5. Don't land on or under the net

As a newer player, you may not be getting as many sets, so it's really tempting to hit as many spikes as you can. This is a great attitude, however, make sure you maintain a controlled hitting approach, and good spatial awareness of the net, including the area under the net.

Many times, players are so focussed on hitting the ball, they don't realize how close to the net they are getting. Remember, touching the net is a rule violation, and can cost your team a point. Even more importantly, however, is the safety aspect. If you're landing in the net, or under the net, there's a good chance you might land on someone else's foot.

So, even though it's tempting to concentrate wholly on hitting the ball, remember to also work on your spatial awareness of how close you are getting to the net.

6. Don't pass the ball too close to the net

Another classic error is to pass (or bump) the ball too close to the net. This is sometimes referred to as an over bump. An over bump makes it really difficult for the setter to be able to set the ball – and even if they can salvage it to get a set, chances are they won't be able to run any plays.

Another reason not to bump too close to the net is that you might inadvertently be setting up the other team. Sometimes an over bump actually does go OVER the net – and if a player from the other team just happens to be in the right position, they may just be able to time a really nice hit. For their team, of course.

To avoid over bumps, when you're passing the ball, try to aim for about a foot off the net. This gives the setter some room. And you, as the passer, some leeway in your target.

7. Don't catch the ball during a play

Okay, this one seems silly. Anyone who knows the rules of volleyball knows that you're not supposed to catch the ball. However, if you've ever been at a volleyball game, especially a volleyball tournament, you'll notice how LOUD it is. There's players yelling, shoes squeaking on the gym floor, volleyballs bouncing, and referees on multiple courts blowing their whistles.

In all this commotion, it's easy for a player to THINK they heard the whistle blow, and to catch the ball to end the play. However, if you even have a tiny little doubt about whether or not you heard the whistle blow, KEEP PLAYING! Believe me, you will look a lot more foolish if you catch the ball during an active play than if you kept playing after the whistle was blown!

Eventually, the players will figure it out, or the ref will blow their whistle again, and the play will end for real.

8. Always bring all the equipment you're going to need – and maybe even some extra

Volleyball gear

Sure, it's easy to forget to bring something every now and then. Happens to the best of us, in fact. However, don't let it happen consistently. Make a point of using a checklist or packing your bag when you're not in a rush, so that you can review to make sure you've got everything you need.

There are somethings that you can borrow – clean socks, clean shorts, for example. And there are some things that you probably don't want to share – for example, a water bottle, or a sweat towel.

9. Clean your gear!

Speaking of gear, make sure you're cleaning it regularly. Of course, you're going to wash your sports clothes. But I'm talking about your knee pads and ankle braces. After a game, don't just throw them in your bag until next week's game. Make sure that you're airing them out and giving them a wash when they need it. YOU may not notice the odor, but trust me, volleyball gear can get NASTY if you don't care for it!

10. Don't wear the wrong gear

When you're starting a new sport, it's common to not have all the gear right from the start. You want to make sure that you actually enjoy the sport before you commit to buying gear that might be expensive. However, with volleyball, there are a couple things that you'll want to keep in mind regarding gear, that probably won't cost you any extra money.

Volleyball is a court sport, which means that you're going to want to wear indoor shoes. Even if you're not buying specific volleyball shoes right away, do make sure that you're not wearing outdoor shoes on the court. Any dirt or water that is tracked onto the playing surface can be a hazard, as it can cause players to slip when they're running for the ball. They're going to be looking up at the ball, not down at the ground.

Indoor shoes should also be non-marking, so that the rubber doesn't leave any skid marks on the gym floor.

Knee pads aren't mandatory, but they sometimes give new players a bit more confidence when diving for a ball. Just remember, however, that proper diving technique actually doesn't mean dropping to your knees to bump. You should have more of a forward motion.

Volleyball players tend to wear gym clothes that are more fitted than baggy. That's often because you can get called for a net violation even if it's your clothes that touched the net. You don't have to wear a full spandex suit, but think about wearing more fitted, rather than baggy, gym clothes.

11. Don't just jump straight up when blocking

Many people think that when you're blocking a spike, you just put your arms in the air and jump straight up. What you actually want to do is press your hands forward at the peak of your jump, as if you're

pushing against the volleyball as it's being spiked. This push will actually give you a much stronger block and should prevent the momentum of the ball from just pushing right through your hands.

Just make sure that you're jumping high enough over the net, so that you're pushing above the height of the net and not touching the net at all – otherwise you might be at risk of getting a net violation call.

12. Don't get a foot violation when serving

Serving is the only time you get to start a play with complete control of the ball. So, you would think that no one would ever get a foot violation, since the player gets to decide how much room they need for their serve. While it doesn't happen often, getting a foot violation when you're serving is kind of embarrassing. And it doesn't happen to just new players – experienced players can also misjudge where they're standing when they start their serve. But regardless of how long you've been playing, when you hear the whistle blow on a foot violation, it's a total "d'oh" moment.

The best way to avoid this embarrassing call is to always take a look at the lines when you go back to serve, and make sure you're starting back enough to give you the amount of room you need. You might also want to practice your serve outside of a game situation, so that you can judge how much room you need to serve, and get really comfortable with that amount of space.

13. Make sure you have a defensive position

A defensive position is the stance you take when the other team is getting ready to set up an attack and spike the ball over. Having a good defensive position means you can respond to that attack as quickly as possible.

Standing with your arms clasped in front of you and legs straight is not a defensive position. This is a spectating position. A good defensive position means that the player's arms are bent in front of them, so they can move quickly in any direction to respond to where the ball is going. The player's legs are bent, they are bent forward at the waist, and they are leaning forward slightly. This forward lean is where the term, "on your toes" comes from.

Being in a good defensive position is more than just being able to respond physically to the ball. It's also being mentally ready to respond as well, and being able to anticipate where the ball is going. When a player is in a good defensive position, they're recognizing that the ball may come towards them, and they're ready to respond to it.

14. Always be ready for the ball

With 6 players on the court, and only 3 touches per play, that means that for every play there's a minimum of 3 players who don't get to touch the ball before it goes over. If you're one of the 6 players on the court, don't get caught spectating instead of playing! You never know when there's going to be a bad pass that has be to run down, when a non-setter player has to set the ball, or which hitter is going to get the set.

One of the most common ways of not being ready for the ball is for back-court players to not be ready to get a set. A back-court player could get a set because of a bad pass, or it could be a strategic set to mix up the attack. So, even when you're in the back court, remember that back-court players can still get a set! Always be ready, even if it seems like you're not going to be in the play.

15. Make sure you warm up

So many times, I've seen recreational league athletes arrive at a game late, rush to tie their shoes, and just jump on the court to play, without any kind of warmup. Putting on your indoor shoes definitely does not count as a warmup.

A good warmup prepares muscles and ligaments to be used more strenuously for the upcoming physical activity, for two main purposes: 1) to contribute to better performance; and 2) to help prevent injury.

The irony is, as you get older, you actually NEED to warmup even more. Muscles, joints, and ligaments may not be as pliable as they used to be, and not giving them a good warmup makes them more susceptible to injury.

Getting injured is never a good thing. Not only can it prevent you from playing your favorite sports and activities, it can sideline you from your daily responsibilities as well. And, studies have shown older athletes can actually take longer to recover from an injury than younger athletes.

So, take the time to give yourself a good warm up to prepare for the game. A good practice is to consider the time you need for a warmup as just part of the total time required for the activity. For example, if game start is 7:30, make sure you get to the gym at 7:00, which gives you plenty of time to get your gear on and include a warmup.

16. And don't forget to cool down, too!

Even though it's tempting to head out for post-game bevvys right after the game is over, having a good cool down is just as important as a good warmup. This is when your muscles and ligaments are nice and warm, so doing a few good stretches will help the lactic acid from settling in and will help prevent soreness.

A cool down doesn't have to be complicated. Just include a few key stretches, really focusing on the muscles you've really used during the game. You can also use this time to chat with your teammates about how the game went – and to tease any teammates who got a foot violation when they served the ball!

Keep these tips in mind the next time you hit the volleyball court. Even if you don't have years of experience playing volleyball, these tips will help you feel more at home on the court.

Made in the USA
Columbia, SC
03 April 2025